1 MONTH OF FREE READING

at

www.ForgottenBooks.com

By purchasing this book you are eligible for one month membership to ForgottenBooks.com, giving you unlimited access to our entire collection of over 1,000,000 titles via our web site and mobile apps.

To claim your free month visit: www.forgottenbooks.com/free1177323

* Offer is valid for 45 days from date of purchase. Terms and conditions apply.

ISBN 978-0-331-46755-0
PIBN 11177323

This book is a reproduction of an important historical work. Forgotten Books uses state-of-the-art technology to digitally reconstruct the work, preserving the original format whilst repairing imperfections present in the aged copy. In rare cases, an imperfection in the original, such as a blemish or missing page, may be replicated in our edition. We do, however, repair the vast majority of imperfections successfully; any imperfections that remain are intentionally left to preserve the state of such historical works.

Forgotten Books is a registered trademark of FB &c Ltd.
Copyright © 2018 FB &c Ltd.
FB &c Ltd, Dalton House, 60 Windsor Avenue, London, SW19 2RR.
Company number 08720141. Registered in England and Wales.

For support please visit www.forgottenbooks.com

Historic, Archive Document

Do not assume content reflects current scientific knowledge, policies, or practices.

FALL OF 1929

CASHTOWN NURSERIES

E. W. HARTMAN, Proprietor

ESTABLISHED 1856

CASHTOWN, PA.

(ADAMS COUNTY)

COMMONWEALTH OF PENNSYLVANIA
DEPARTMENT OF AGRICULTURE
Bureau of Plant Industry
NURSERY CERTIFICATE NO. 99 (RESIDENT)

THIS IS TO CERTIFY THAT THE NURSERY PREMIS[ES] Cashtown Nurseries, E. W. Hartman, Prop., Cashtown, Pa., including 25 a[cres] stock have been officially inspected and passed in accordance with the pro[visions] of Act of the General Assembly, approved the 10th day of March, 1927.

Permission is hereby granted this nursery to sell and ship nursery [stock] which has been officially inspected, for the year ending September 30th[,] provided that a tag on which an exact copy of this certificate is printed [is] attached to each package, bundle, bale, box or carload lot so shipped.

This certificate does not cover the requirements of any special quara[ntine] regulation promulgated by this Commonwealth or by the United States [Depart]ment of Agriculture.

This certificate is void after October 1, 1929, but may be revoked for [cause.]

Issued at the State Capitol, Harrisburg, Pa., August 10, 1929.

F. M. TRIMBLE, Chief Nursery Inspector.   R. H. BELL, [

NOTICE TO PURCHASERS

We use the greatest care to have our stock reliable and [true to] name, and will on proper proof, replace anything that may no[t prove] true to name. We do not give any warranty. It is mutually [agreed] between the purchaser and ourselves, that we shall not at a[ny time] be held responsible from any cause for more than the origin[al cost] of the trees.

APPLE TREES

CAN FURNISH OTHER VARITIES NOT LISTED

Prices on Apple Trees 2 Years Old

	Each	Per 10	Per 100	Per 1000
First Class 5 to 6 ft.	50c	45c	35c	30c
First Class 4 to 5 ft.	45c	40c	30c	25c
First Class 3 to 4 ft.	30c	30c	20c	18c

PRICES OF 1 YEAR APPLE TREES

	Each	Per 10	Per 100	Per 1000
4 to 5 ft.	40c	35c	25c	20c
3 to 4 ft.	35c	30c	20c	18c
2 to 3 ft.	25c	25c	18c	15c

These are a fine lot in apple trees. Nice clean, thrifty trees, well grown. Varieties are here given and time of ripening.

Yellow Transparent. Earliest and best, white, tender, juicy, sprightly, sub-acid, grows upright, bears young, making good filler, July 1st to 15th.

Early Ripe. Of good fair size, pale yellow, ripens little later than early harvest.

Duchess of Oldenburg. Good large size golden streaked red, sub-acid, fine shipper and market apple, last of July.

Wealthy. Good medium size, round or pointed, almost solid red, flesh white, crisp, juicy, bears young, August 1st to 15th.

Summer Rambo. Very large in size, greenish red striped, tender, juicy, tree strong grower, August 15th to September 15th.

Smoke House. One of the good old kind welcomed in every home. Ripens in September and can be kept in common storage late into the winter.

Grimes Golden. Of good size, yellow, of high quality, ripens in September, can be kept late into the winter.

Jonathan. Very red, smooth, of good size, fine quality, ripens in September, can be kept in common storage late in the winter.

McIntosh. Bright, deep red, fine quality, ripens in September and keeps late into the winter in common storage.

Stayman Winesap. Large size, mostly covered red, crisp and juicy, tree a strong grower, said to be one of the best apples for orchard planting east of the Mississippi, ripen in October and ready for use soon after picking, keeps late into spring.

York Imperial. Winter, medium to large, yellow shaded red, firm, juicy, sub-acid, an excellent canning and shipping apple, one of the good apples for export, October.

Discount of 5% on all orders received, accompanied with cash on or before March 1, 1930.

Rome Beauty. Winter, large, round, mottled and striped in different shades of red, flavor and quality fine. Good late keeper.

Delicious. (Sometimes called the Stark's Delicious), Winter apple, one of the fine quality apples. Brilliant dark red shading to yellow at the blossom end, growing somewhat in quince shape, very attractive.

Paradise Winter Sweet. Large, creamy, rosy cheeked, one of the best sweet winter varieties.

Winter Banana. Yellow with pink cheek, classes as a winter apple, a fancy apple.

Black Ben. A dark red winter apple, good commercial apple.

Maiden Blush. A good early variety. Splendid apple for house use.

Gravenstine. A full variety, ripening after Summer Rambo, Commercial variety.

Cortland. An improved McIntosh that comes from Geneva N. Y., and considered second to none.

Baldwin. An old standard that needs no description.

Northern Spy. This is a large fall to late winter apple, good variety.

Early Harvest. An early market variety, ripening between Yellow Transparent and Early Ripe, good bearer.

Hubertson. Late fall or early winter, classed as commercial variety, Heavy bearer.

M. B. Twig. One of the winter varieties of the winesap family. Popular in many fruit grown sections.

Wm. E. Red. An early red apple, ripening August 10 to 15, commercial variety.

King of Tompkins Co. Large red apple, quality 1st class.

Gano. An improved Ben Davis.

Loveland Raspberry. An early red apple of good quality.

Pound. An old variety, very large, once very popular.

King David. Late fall and winter variety, dark red, used as an Export apple.

(2)

TRUE TO NAME, OUR AIM.

Budding Peach Trees, one of the most particular operations in nursery work.

PEACH TREES
CAN FURNISH OTHER VARIETIES OF PEACH NOT LISTED.

Peach	Each	Per 10	Per 100	Per 1000
5 to 6 ft.	40c	35c	20c	18c
4 to 5 ft.	35c	30c	18c	16c
3 to 4 ft.	30c	25c	16c	15c
2 to 3 ft.	25c	20c	12c	12c

These peach trees are an exceptionally fine lot of trees of good large size, healthy and thrifty and are sure to please. Order of ripening is here given.

Carman. Large creamy white skin, covered mostly red, tender, juicy, good commercial shipper, July 15th to August 1st.

Hiley (Hiley Early Bell). Ripens last of July. This peach is of large size, with delightful red cheek, flesh is white, tender and exceedingly juicy. Free. It is one of the best shippers among early peaches and invariably brings top prices.

Champion. A large handsome, early variety, creamy white with red cheek, sweet, rich and juicy, hardy and productive, August 1st.

Bell of Georgia. Very large, in white with red cheek, flesh white and firm, excellent flavor, fine shipper, August 1st to 15th.

Special prices to Co-Operative Associations.

Mountain Rose. Large red, flesh white, juicy, excellent, one of the best, August 1st to 15th.

Southaven. A yellow peach ripening before Elberta. Considered one of the best varieties.

Elberta. One of the greatest commercial yellow peaches known, good shipper. Tree hardy and good grower, Aug. 15th to Sept. 1st.

Shipper's Late Red. One of the finest yellow peaches grown. As large as Hale, but a much better bearer. Ripens ten days after the Elberta.

Late Elberta. A real Elberta ripening ten days later.

Rex. Fine yellow variety, mid-season.

McAlister. A late yellow peach, good shipper, ripening after, most all commercial varieties, heavy bearer.

J. H. Hale. Larger than Elberta, one of the newer yellow varieties claimed by many to be one of the finest flavored peaches. Ripens little later than Elberta.

Crawfords Late. Large yellow, fine canning and market peach, Sept. 1st. to 15th.

Boers Smock. One of the large yellow peaches, good canning peach, Sept. 15th to Oct. 1st.

Fordes Late. White, one of the good late white peaches, Sept. 15th to Oct. 1st.

Iron Mountain. One of the fine white late peaches, splendid market peach. Tree hardy, strong grower, Sept. 20th to Oct. 1st.

Salway. One of the good late yellow varieties, good canning peach. Latter part of September to October 15th.

BLOCK OF 1 YEAR PEACH TREES

Not how cheap we can grow them, But how Good.

PEAR TREES

STANDARD PEAR TREES

Extra selected, 5 to 6 ft. high, each, $1.00; per 10, $9.00; per 100, $85.00.

VARIETIES OF STANDARD PEARS

Bartlett. Large buttery, juicy, high flavored, great bearer. This sort has long been considered one of the choicest canning varieties, as well as favorite for all other uses, Aug. and Sept.

Claps Favorite. Very large, yellow and dull red, with russet specks, melting rich, August.

Seckel. Small, skin rich yellowish brown, when fully ripe, with deep brownish red cheek; flesh very fine grained, sweet, juicy, melting, buttery; one of the richest and highest flavored pears. Equally popular for dessert and picking. September, October.

Kieffer. Large size, handsome appearance and remarkable keeping qualities. Fine for making butter and canning.

Anjou. Large buttery, melting, rich, vinous. The best late fall and early winter pear. October to January.

Koonce. Medium, yellow with carmine cheek. A profitable early market variety. July.

CHERRY TREES

Extra select, 5 to 6 ft. high, per tree, $1.00; per 10, $9.00, per 100, $75.00.

SWEET
VARIETIES OF CHERRY TREES

Black Tartarian. Very large, dark red cherry, becoming black when over ripe, sweet, juicy, June.

Governor Wood. Large, light red, juicy, rich, delicious. Tree healthy and productive, sweet, June.

Napoleon. Large, pale yellow or red, firm juicy, sweet and productive, July.

Windsor. Large, liver colored, flesh remarkable, firm and of fine quality, tree hardy and prolific. A valuable late sweet variety, July.

Bing. Large red, one of the best market sorts.

SOUR

	Each	Per 10	Per 100	Per 1,000
5 to 6 ft.	75c	65c	50c	45c
4 to 5 ft.	65c	60c	45c	35c
3 to 4 ft.	50c	45c	35c	27½c

Large Montmorency. Large, red, productive, one of the best varieties of sour cherries.

Baldwin. Large, round, slightly sub-acid, sweetest and richest of the sour varieties, June.

Early Richmond. Medium, dark red, melting, juicy, sprightly, rich, acid, June.

Dyehouse. A sure bearer, largely planted for early market; ripening week before Early Richmond, which it closely resembles, June.

PLUM TREES

PLUM TREES 1 YEAR OLD

4 to 6 ft. high, per tree, 85c; per 10, $8.00; per 100, $75.00

Abundance. One of the greatbearers, fruits of lemon to red color, sweet and juicy, August.

Burbank. Most profitable among growers for market ripens 10 to 14 days later than Abundance, cherry red.

German Prune. Large, dark purple, sweet, good, one of the most desirable for canning, September.

Red June. One of the vigorous, upright growers, productive fair size. Vermillion red, ripens a week ahead of Abundance.

Satsuma. A Japan variety, red flesh. Best of Japanese Varieties.

Wickson. Large yellow. Good bearer.

APRICOT TREES 1 YEAR OLD

4 to 6 ft. high, per tree, 80c each.

Early Golden. Orange color, juicy and sweet.

QUINCE TREES

QUINCE TREES 2 YEARS OLD

4 to 6 ft. high, each, $1.00; per 10, $9.00; per 100, $85.00.

VARIETIES OF QUINCE TREES

Orange. Fruit large, bright yellow, of excellent quality.

Champion. A prolific and constant bearer, oval fruit, averaging larger than Orange and long keeper, later than Orange.

Meech Prolific. A vigorous grower and immensely productive, fruit large, orange yellow, delightful flavor, fine cooking qualities.

Plant 15 to 18 feet apart.

GRAPE STALKS

GRAPE STALKS 1 AND 2 YEARS OLD

25c each; per 10, $2.00; per 100, $12.00.

VARIETIES OF GRAPES

Brighton. High quality, handsome, large, one of the most popular reds.

Concord. The leading market, vineyard and home garden variety, dark blue, fine quality.

Delaware. The exquisite little American dessert grape, very highest quality.

Green Mountain. Probably finest quality in this class, a home garden variety, not profitable commercially, ripens very early.

Worden. Resembles Concord, but is sweeter, larger in bunches and berry, week to 10 days earlier than Concord.

Niagara. The standard white grape, bunches and berries larger than Concord, very sweet, ripens with Concord.

Moor's Early. Bunch medium, berry large round, vine exceedingly hardy, ripens 3 weeks ahead of the Concord, desirable for early market.

Plant 6 to 8 feet apart in rows, making rows 8 feet apart.

CURRANT STALKS
CURRANT STALKS 1 AND 2 YEARS OLD

40c each; per 10, $3.50; per 100, $30.00.

Perfection. Beautiful, bright red, very productive, one of the best home and market varieties.

Fay. One of the long leading market varieties for garden and market, red variety.

Plant 4 to 6 feet apart.

Miscellaneous Small Fruits
GOOSEBERRIES 1 AND 2 YEARS OLD

40c each; per 10, $3.50; per 100, $30.00.

Downing. Large, handsome, pale green and of splendid quality for both cooking and table use, bush a vigorous grower and usually free from mildew.

Josselyn. Large size, smooth, prolific and hardy, wonderful croper with bright, clean, healthy foliage.

Plant 3 to 4 feet apart.

RASPBERRIES

.50c per 10; per 100, $3.50.

Cumberland. A healthy, vigorous grower, growing up stout, stalky, well branched canes that produce immense crops of magnificent berries, fruit very large, firm, the most profitable market variety, mid season.

Plum Farmer. One of the profitable early black varieties of good size.

St. Regis. A genuine, practical, profitable, continuous to fall bearing red raspberry. Fruit begins to ripen with the earliest and continues on young canes to October.

Plant in rows 5 feet apart and 3 feet in rows.

BLACKBERRIES

Each, 15c; per 10, $1.00; per 100, $9.00.

Eldorado. Stalks are vigorous and hardy enduring the winter. Berries large, jet black, borne in large clusters and ripen well together, very sweet and melting and pleasant to the taste, have no hard core and keep 8 to 10 days after picking in good condition.

Snyder. Enormously productive, medium sweet, no hard sour core, the leading variety where hardiness is the consideration, ripens early.

Plant rows 6 to 7 feet apart, 3 to 4 ft. rows.

STRAWBERRIES

100, $1.50; 1000, $12.00.

Gandy.   Wm. Belt.   Chespeake.   Premier.   Corsican.

ASPARAGUS 1 AND 2 YEARS OLD

100, $2.00; 1000, $15.00.

Conovers. A standard variety of large size, tender and excellent quality.

Palmetto. A very early variety, even regular size of excellent quality.

Washington. Rust proof. Large and one of the best varieties.

Plant in rich soil, dig trench and set in 12 to 18 inches apart, covering crown 2 inches below surface.

EVERGREENS

American Arborvitae. Foliage bright green. Branches short and horizontal, forming a narrow pyramidal tree. Used for screens and hedges. 2 to 3 feet $2.75 each, 3 to 4 feet $4.00 each.

Arborvitae Globossa. A perfect globe, very desirable for bedding and formal use. Light green in foliage. 15 to 18 in. $2.75 each, 18 to 24 in. $3.50 each.

Golden Arborvitae. Bright yellow overlies the green foliage. Tall and columnar in habit, valuable in grouping with green kinds. 15 to 18 in. $3.00 each, 18 to 24 in. $3.25 each.

Hovey Golden. Fine green foliage tipped with yellow. For window boxes and hedges. 15 to 18 in. $2.25 each, 18 to 24 in. $2.75 each.

Pyramidal Arborvitae. Upright habit a great improvement over American, as it is more dense in foliage. Best arborvitae for general purposes. 18 to 24 in. $3.50 each, 2 to 3 ft. $4.00 each, 3 to 4 ft. $5.00 each.

Siberian Arborvitae. Very satisfactory dwarf evergreen specimen. The foliage remains a rich dark green all year, very hardy. 15 to 18 in. $2.75 each, 18 to 24 in. $3.50 each.

Irish Juniper. The foliage is glaucous green, it is very slender in habit of growth and needs no shearing. 18 to 24 in. $2.25, 2 to 3 feet $2.75.

We are in a position to make your planting plan.

EVERGREENS---Continued

Pfitzariana Juniper. A wide growing and very graceful evergreen, foliage bluish green. Will grow upright if trained. 15 to 18 in. $4.00 each, 18 to 24 in. $4.50 each.

Sabina Juniper. A low spreading tree with handsome, dark green foliage, very hardy, suitable for lawns and cemeteries. 15 to 18 in. $2.75 each, 18 to 24 in. $3.50 each.

Virginiana Glauca Juniper. Silvery blue foliage, tall and slender habit, very hardy. 18 to 24 in. $3.75 each, 2 to 3 ft. $4.50 each.

Mugho Pine. A very compact, globular tree of pleasing form, very desirable. 12 to 15 in. $3.00 each, 15 to 18 in. $3.50 each.

Retinspora Plumosa. The young foliage is very light green bordering on yellow. For foundation and lawn planting it is one of the most popular. 15 to 18 in $2.75 each, 18 to 24 in. $3.25 each.

Retinspora Squarossa. The foliage of this is very fine cut. In foliage it is a very pleasing blue. You can shear to any shape you want. 15 to 18 in. $2.50 each, 18 to 24 in. $3.00 each.

Retinspora Aurea. Dwarf, upright in habit the most beautiful golden Retinspora. 12 to 15 in. $3.50 each.

Elwangeriana Rengold. Dwarf in habit, very yellow in foliage. A freak among the evergreens. 12 to 15 in. $3.50 each.

Austrian Pine. Of strong, spreading growth and rounded form; regularly arranged branches. 3 ft. $4.00, 4 to 5 ft. $6.00.

Hemlock Pine. A graceful tree, hardy, fine for moist places. Branches droop, making a striking appearance. 2 to 3 ft. $3.50, 3 to 4 ft. $4.50.

Black Hills Spruce. Similar to Norway, but thicker in the foliage and much more desirable. 2 to 3 ft. $3.50, 3 to 4 ft. $4.50.

White Spruce. Growing similar to a Norway, but with a white foliage. 18 to 24 in. $3.00 each, 2 to 3 ft. $3.75 each.

Colorado Blue. Silvery blue of vigorous growth. Hardy in any exposure. 18 to 24 ln., $8.00.

Kosters Blue. The best blue spruce obtainable, and looked upon as the very choicest evergreen growth. 15 to 18 in., $10 each.

Norway Spruce. The most popular of the spruce family, easy to transplant and grows rapidly. 18 to 24 in $2.50 each, 2 to 3 ft. $3.25 each.

We can furnish larger and smaller evergreens.
Write for prices.

ROSES
Everblooming Hybrid Teas

	Each	Per 10
Columbia Pink	.90	.75
Dutchess of Wellington, Coppery Yellow	.90	.75
Francis Scott Key, Crimson Red	.90	.75
General McArthur, Scarlet	.90	.75
Killarney, Pink	.90	.75
Sunburst, Yellow	.90	.75
Los Angeles, Coral	.90	.75
White Killarney, White	.90	.75

Any six of the above roses sent Parcel Post $4.25.

Climbing and Rambler Roses

	Each	Per 10
American Pillar, Pink	.75	.65
Dorthy Perkins, White	.75	.65
American Beauty, Pink	.75	.65
Flower of Fairfield, Crimson	.75	.65
Excelsa, Red	.75	.65

DECIDUOUS TREES

	Each	Per 10
CATALAPA—Bungei 1 yr., 6 to 7 feet	$2.75	$25.00
" " 2 yr., 6 to 7 feet	3.50	30.00
MAPLE—Norway 6 to 8 feet	2.00	17.50
" " 8 to 10 feet	2.50	20.00
" Silver 6 to 8 feet	1.75	15.00
" " 8 to 10 feet	2.25	20.00
" Sugar or Rock 8 to 10 feet	2.50	22.50
BIRCH—Cut Leaf Weeping (snowy white) 4 to 5 feet	2.75	
" " " " " " 5 to 6 feet	3.00	

CHINESE OR SIBERIAN ELM

This tree was introduced in 1908 by Frank N. Meyer. Agricultural explorer, from near Peaking. It is a fine case of the survival of the fittest, for it has not only maintained its existence through centuries under the most adverse soil and climatic conditions. But has thrived and made a luxurious growth. Home owners, Real Estate men, and others interested in securing quick shade with a minimum of time and expense will find in this tree the characteristics they desire. Its Habit of growth makes it an ideal tree for city street planting, or for shade around the home in either city or country. The tree is healthy, thrifty, and beautiful, and will give abundant shade in short time. A one year tree 5 ft. in four years from planting produced a tree measuring: Circumference 20 in., Height 20 ft., Spread 18 ft.

	Each	Per 10	Per 25
7 to 8 ft.	1.75	15.00	33.75

DECIDUOUS SHRUBS

ALMONDS—White 18 to 24 in.	$1.00 each
" " 2 to 3 ft.	1.50 each
" " 3 to 4 ft.	2.25 each
" Pink 18 to 24 in.	1.00 each
" " 2 to 3 ft.	1.50 each
ALTHEA—Asst. 2 to 3 ft.	$ .75 each
" " 3 to 4 ft.	1.00 each
NEW RED BARBERRY—1 yr.	$1.00
" " " 2 yr.	1.25
BARBERRY—Thumbergii 18 to 24 in. per 10	$2.00
" " 24 to 30 in. per 10	3.00

CALIFORNIA PRIVET, 2 yr.—

	Per 100	Per 1000
15 to 18 in.	$3.00	$25.00
18 to 24 in.	4.00	35.00

BUTTERFLY BUSH—2 to 3 ft.	.90 each
HYDRANGEA—Arborescens Grand 18 to 24 in.	$ .75 each
" " " 2 to 3 ft.	.90 each
" Paniculata Grand 18 -24 in.	.75 each
" " " 2 to 3 ft.	.90 each
" Tree form 2 to 3 ft.	1.00 each
" " " 3 to 4 ft.	1.25 each
FRENCH HYDRANGEA—Blue 18 to 24 in.	$1.00 each
" " Pink 18 to 24 in.	1.00 each
LILAC—Purple 18 to 24 in.	$ .75 each
" " 2 to 3 ft.	1.00 each
" White 2 to 3 ft.	.75 each
" " 3 to 4 ft.	1.00 each
PHILADELPHUS—Aurea 2 to 3 ft.	$ .75 each
PHILADELPHUS CORONARIUS—(Sweet scented Mock Orange) 2 to 3 ft.	$ .75 each
PLUM—Purple 2 to 3 ft.	$ .75 each
" " 3 to 4 ft.	1.00 each
SPIREA—Anthony Waterer 12 to 15 in.	$ .50 each
" " 15 to 18 in.	.60 each
" Billardii 18 to 24 in.	.50 each
" " 2 to 3 ft.	.60 each
" Thumbergii 12 to 15 in.	.50 each
" " 15 to 18 in.	.60 each
" Van Houttei 15 to 18 in.	.40 each
" " " 18 to 24 in.	.50 each
WEIGELIA—Desboisi 2 to 3 ft.	$ .50 each
" " 3 to 4 ft.	.75 each
" Eva Rathke 2 to 3 ft.	.75 each
" " 3 to 4 ft.	1.00 each

CLIMBING VINES

DUTCHMAN'S PIPE—2 yr.	$1.50 each
HONEYSUCKLE—Halliana, 2 yr.	.75 each
CLEMATIS HYBRIDS—Jackmanii, Blue, 2 yr.	1.00 each
CLEMATIS EDOUARD AUDRE—Red, 2 yr.	1.00 each
WISTERIA SINENSIS—2 yr.	.75 each

TO WHOM IT MAY CONCERN

This nursery business was established by N. W. Hartman in the year 1856 and known as the Fairview Nurseries until the death of the above named 1898. After this date it was reorganized and named Cashtown Nurseries and operated by E. W. Hartman, son of N. W. Hartman.

TO THE PLANTERS INTERESTS

We have in connection with our nursery, bearing orchards of several hundred acres and cut our buds and cions from these orchards and know that we are able to give the planter the variety or varieties for which he asks.

The work of cutting the buds and cions is in all cases done by one of the men associated with the business. It is plain to the orchard planter, that by our plan of working from bearing orchards each year gives a decided advantage over the nurseryman who is obliged cut buds etc., from his growing stock year after year.

OUR PRICES

We wish to state, that in presenting this price-list with a brief description of stock listed, that we are trying to save money for the planter. It is a known fact that the purchaser, in all cases must pay for the advertising, whether it be a small leaflet, as this one or an elaborate catalogue with colored plates and cuts that are often misleading.

Our trade is largely with the commercial planter who buys from us year after year. If it is good business for the large planter to buy from us, it is also wise for the small planter, to do likewise.

Yours very truly,

E. W. HARTMAN.

TERMS

A cash deposit of 20 per cent. on all orders for $5.00 and over. Cash with all orders for $5.00 and less. All orders prepaid when cash in full accompanies order.

PACKING OF NURSERY STOCK

Will be done in boxes or in bales, protecting the roots and trees well in shipping. These prices include the packing, delivered on board cars Gettysburg and Chambersburg. No charges for packing or delivering to railroad.

Will accept all orders upon condition that they shall be void should any injury befall the stock from hail, storm or other causes over which I have no control.

RESPONSIBILITY

All articles after being delivered to railroad in good condition are at the risk of the purchaser.

Certificate of Nursery Inspection accompanies each shipment of nursery stock.

SHIPPING

Purchasers are requested to state whether they wish stock shipped by freight or express.

CASHTOWN NURSERIES
CASHTOWN, PA.

Lightning Source UK Ltd.
Milton Keynes UK
UKHW020757270219
338009UK00008B/1770/P